# Great Works Instructional Guide for Literature

# The Odyssey

A guide for the epic poem by Homer
Translated by Robert Fagles
Great Works Author: Jennifer Kroll

SHELL EDUCATION

## Image Credits

Shutterstock (cover; page 1)

## Standards

© 2007 Teachers of English to Speakers of Other Languages, Inc. (TESOL)
© 2007 Board of Regents of the University of Wisconsin System. World-Class Instructional Design and Assessment (WIDA)
© Copyright 2010. National Governors Association Center for Best Practices and Council of Chief State School Officers.
All rights reserved.

---

## Shell Education

5301 Oceanus Drive
Huntington Beach, CA 92649-1030
http://www.shelleducation.com

**ISBN 978-1-4258-8994-4**

© 2015 Shell Educational Publishing, Inc.

# Table of Contents

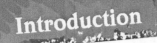 

# How to Use This Literature Guide

Today's standards demand rigor and relevance in the reading of complex texts. The units in this series guide teachers in a rich and deep exploration of worthwhile works of literature for classroom study. The most rigorous instruction can also be interesting and engaging!

Many current strategies for effective literacy instruction have been incorporated into these instructional guides for literature. Throughout the units, text-dependent questions are used to determine comprehension of the book as well as student interpretation of the vocabulary words. The books chosen for the series are complex exemplars of carefully crafted works of literature. Close reading is used throughout the units to guide students toward revisiting the text and using textual evidence to respond to prompts orally and in writing. Students must analyze the story elements in multiple assignments for each section of the book. All of these strategies work together to rigorously guide students through their study of literature.

The next few pages will make clear how to use this guide for a purposeful and meaningful literature study. Each section of this guide is set up in the same way to make it easier for you to implement the instruction in your classroom.

## Theme Thoughts

The great works of literature used throughout this series have important themes that have been relevant to people for many years. Many of the themes will be discussed during the various sections of this instructional guide. However, it would also benefit students to have independent time to think about the key themes of the novel.

Before students begin reading, have them complete *Pre-Reading Theme Thoughts* (page 13). This graphic organizer will allow students to think about the themes outside the context of the story. They'll have the opportunity to evaluate statements based on important themes and defend their opinions. Be sure to have students keep their papers for comparison to the *Post-Reading Theme Thoughts* (page 64). This graphic organizer is similar to the pre-reading activity. However, this time, students will be answering the questions from the point of view of one of the characters in the novel. They have to think about how the character would feel about each statement and defend their thoughts. To conclude the activity, have students compare what they thought about the themes before they read the novel to what the characters discovered during the story.

# How to Use This Literature Guide (cont.)

## Vocabulary

Each teacher overview page has definitions and sentences about how key vocabulary words are used in the section. These words should be introduced and discussed with students. There are two student vocabulary activity pages in each section. On the first page, students are asked to define the ten words chosen by the author of this unit. On the second page in most sections, each student will select at least eight words that he or she finds interesting or difficult. For each section, choose one of these pages for your students to complete. With either assignment, you may want to have students get into pairs to discuss the meanings of the words. Allow students to use reference guides to define the words. Monitor students to make sure the definitions they have found are accurate and relate to how the words are used in the text.

On some of the vocabulary student pages, students are asked to answer text-related questions about the vocabulary words. The following question stems will help you create your own vocabulary questions if you'd like to extend the discussion.

- How does this word describe _____'s character?
- In what ways does this word relate to the problem in this story?
- How does this word help you understand the setting?
- In what ways is this word related to the story's solution?
- Describe how this word supports the novel's theme of . . . .
- What visual images does this word bring to your mind?
- For what reasons might the author have chosen to use this particular word?

At times, more work with the words will help students understand their meanings. The following quick vocabulary activities are a good way to further study the words.

- Have students practice their vocabulary and writing skills by creating sentences and/or paragraphs in which multiple vocabulary words are used correctly and with evidence of understanding.
- Students can play vocabulary concentration. Students make a set of cards with the words and a separate set of cards with the definitions. Then, students lay the cards out on the table and play concentration. The goal of the game is to match vocabulary words with their definitions.
- Students can create word journal entries about the words. Students choose words they think are important and then describe why they think each word is important within the novel.

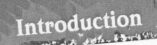
# How to Use This Literature Guide (cont.)

## Analyzing the Literature

After students have read each section, hold small-group or whole-class discussions. Questions are written at two levels of complexity to allow you to decide which questions best meet the needs of your students. The Level 1 questions are typically less abstract than the Level 2 questions. Level 1 is indicated by a square, while Level 2 is indicated by a triangle. These questions focus on the various story elements, such as character, setting, and plot. Student pages are provided if you want to assign these questions for individual student work before your group discussion. Be sure to add further questions as your students discuss what they've read. For each question, a few key points are provided for your reference as you discuss the novel with students.

## Reader Response

In today's classrooms, there are often great readers who are below-average writers. So much time and energy is spent in classrooms getting students to read on grade level that little time is left to focus on writing skills. To help teachers include more writing in their daily literacy instruction, each section of this guide has a literature-based reader response prompt. Each of the three genres of writing is used in the reader responses within this guide: narrative, informative/explanatory, and argument. Students have a choice between two prompts for each reader response. One response requires students to make connections between the reading and their own lives. The other prompt requires students to determine text-to-text connections or connections within the text.

## Close Reading the Literature

Within each section, students are asked to closely reread a short section of text. Since some versions of the novels have different page numbers, the selections are described by chapter and location, along with quotations to guide the readers. After each close reading, there are text-dependent questions to be answered by students.

Encourage students to read each question one at a time and then go back to the text and discover the answer. Work with students to ensure that they use the text to determine their answers rather than making unsupported inferences. Once students have answered the questions, discuss what they discovered. Suggested answers are provided in the answer key.

# How to Use This Literature Guide (cont.)

## Close Reading the Literature (cont.)

The generic, open-ended stems below can be used to write your own text-dependent questions if you would like to give students more practice.

- Give evidence from the text to support . . . .

- Justify your thinking using text evidence about . . . .

- Find evidence to support your conclusions about . . . .

- What text evidence helps the reader understand . . . ?

- Use the book to tell why _____ happens.

- Based on events in the story, . . . .

- Use text evidence to describe why . . . .

## Making Connections

The activities in this section help students make cross-curricular connections to writing, mathematics, science, social studies, or the fine arts. Each of these types of activities requires higher-order thinking skills from students.

## Creating with the Story Elements

It is important to spend time discussing the common story elements in literature. Understanding the characters, setting, and plot can increase students' comprehension and appreciation of the story. If teachers discuss these elements daily, students will more likely internalize the concepts and look for the elements in their independent reading. Another important reason for focusing on the story elements is that students will be better writers if they think about how the stories they read are constructed.

Students are given three options for working with the story elements. They are asked to create something related to the characters, setting, or plot of the novel. Students are given a choice in this activity so that they can decide to complete the activity that most appeals to them. Different multiple intelligences are used so that the activities are diverse and interesting to all students.

# How to Use This Literature Guide (cont.)

## Culminating Activity

This open-ended, cross-curricular activity requires higher-order thinking and allows for a creative product. Students will enjoy getting the chance to share what they have discovered through reading the novel. Be sure to allow them enough time to complete the activity at school or home.

## Comprehension Assessment

The questions in this section are modeled after current standardized tests to help students analyze what they've read and prepare for tests they may see in their classrooms. The questions are dependent on the text and require critical-thinking skills to answer.

## Response to Literature

The final post-reading activity is an essay based on the text that also requires further research by students. This is a great way to extend this book into other curricular areas. A suggested rubric is provided for teacher reference.

# Correlation to the Standards

Shell Education is committed to producing educational materials that are research and standards based. As part of this effort, we have correlated all of our products to the academic standards of all 50 states, the District of Columbia, the Department of Defense Dependents Schools, and all Canadian provinces.

## Purpose and Intent of Standards

Standards are designed to focus instruction and guide adoption of curricula. Standards are statements that describe the criteria necessary for students to meet specific academic goals. They define the knowledge, skills, and content students should acquire at each level. Standards are also used to develop standardized tests to evaluate students' academic progress. Teachers are required to demonstrate how their lessons meet standards. Standards are used in the development of all of our products, so educators can be assured they meet high academic standards.

## How to Find Standards Correlations

To print a customized correlation report of this product for your state, visit our website at http://www.shelleducation.com and follow the online directions. If you require assistance in printing correlation reports, please contact our Customer Service Department at 1-877-777-3450.

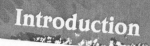

# Correlation to the Standards (cont.)

## Standards Correlation Chart

The lessons in this guide were written to support the Common Core College and Career Readiness Anchor Standards. This chart indicates which sections of this guide address the anchor standards.

| Common Core College and Career Readiness Anchor Standard | Section |
|---|---|
| **CCSS.ELA-Literacy.CCRA.R.1**—Read closely to determine what the text says explicitly and to make logical inferences from it; cite specific textual evidence when writing or speaking to support conclusions drawn from the text. | Close Reading the Literature Sections 1–5; Analyzing the Literature Sections 1–5 |
| **CCSS.ELA-Literacy.CCRA.R.2**—Determine central ideas or themes of a text and analyze their development; summarize the key supporting details and ideas. | Analyzing the Literature Sections 1–5; Post-Reading Response to Literature |
| **CCSS.ELA-Literacy.CCRA.R.3**—Analyze how and why individuals, events, or ideas develop and interact over the course of a text. | Analyzing the Literature Sections 1–5; Making Connections Section 5; Creating with the Story Elements Sections 1–5; Post-Reading Response to Literature |
| **CCSS.ELA-Literacy.CCRA.R.4**—Interpret words and phrases as they are used in a text, including determining technical, connotative, and figurative meanings, and analyze how specific word choices shape meaning or tone. | Vocabulary Sections 1–5; Making Connections Section 3 |
| **CCSS.ELA-Literacy.CCRA.R.5**—Analyze the structure of texts, including how specific sentences, paragraphs, and larger portions of the text (e.g., a section, chapter, scene, or stanza) relate to each other and the whole. | Reader Response Sections 1–5; Making Connections Section 5 |
| **CCSS.ELA-Literacy.CCRA.R.10**—Read and comprehend complex literary and informational texts independently and proficiently. | Entire Unit |
| **CCSS.ELA-Literacy.CCRA.W.1**—Write arguments to support claims in an analysis of substantive topics or texts using valid reasoning and relevant and sufficient evidence. | Reader Response Sections 1–4 |
| **CCSS.ELA-Literacy.CCRA.W.2**—Write informative/explanatory texts to examine and convey complex ideas and information clearly and accurately through the effective selection, organization, and analysis of content. | Reader Response Sections 1–2, 4–5; Culminating Activity 1 |
| **CCSS.ELA-Literacy.CCRA.W.3**—Write narratives to develop real or imagined experiences or events using effective technique, well-chosen details, and well-structured event sequences. | Reader Response Sections 3, 5; Culminating Activity |
| **CCSS.ELA-Literacy.CCRA.W.4**—Produce clear and coherent writing in which the development, organization, and style are appropriate to task, purpose, and audience. | Reader Response Sections 1–5; Culminating Activity |

# Correlation to the Standards (cont.)

## Standards Correlation Chart (cont.)

| Common Core College and Career Readiness Anchor Standard | Section |
|---|---|
| **CCSS.ELA-Literacy.CCRA.W.7**—Conduct short as well as more sustained research projects based on focused questions, demonstrating understanding of the subject under investigation. | Making Connections Section 1 |
| **CCSS.ELA-Literacy.CCRA.W.8**—Gather relevant information from multiple print and digital sources, assess the credibility and accuracy of each source, and integrate the information while avoiding plagiarism. | Making Connections Section 1 |
| **CCSS.ELA-Literacy.CCRA.W.9**—Draw evidence from literary or informational texts to support analysis, reflection, and research. | Close Reading the Literature Sections 1–5; Analyzing the Literature Sections 1–5 |
| **CCSS.ELA-Literacy.CCRA.L.1**—Demonstrate command of the conventions of standard English grammar and usage when writing or speaking. | Reader Response Sections 1–5; Culminating Activity |
| **CCSS.ELA-Literacy.CCRA.L.3**—Apply knowledge of language to understand how language functions in different contexts, to make effective choices for meaning or style, and to comprehend more fully when reading or listening. | Creating with the Story Elements Sections 1–5; Close Reading the Literature Sections 1–5 |
| **CCSS.ELA-Literacy.CCRA.L.4**—Determine or clarify the meaning of unknown and multiple-meaning words and phrases by using context clues, analyzing meaningful word parts, and consulting general and specialized reference materials, as appropriate. | Vocabulary Sections 1–5 |
| **CCSS.ELA-Literacy.CCRA.L.5**—Demonstrate understanding of figurative language, word relationships, and nuances in word meanings. | Making Connections Sections 2–3 |
| **CCSS.ELA-Literacy.CCRA.L.6**—Acquire and use accurately a range of general academic and domain-specific words and phrases sufficient for reading, writing, speaking, and listening at the college and career readiness level; demonstrate independence in gathering vocabulary knowledge when encountering an unknown term important to comprehension or expression. | Vocabulary Sections 1–5 |

## TESOL and WIDA Standards

The lessons in this book promote English language development for English language learners. The following TESOL and WIDA English Language Development Standards are addressed through the activities in this book:

- **Standard 1:** English language learners communicate for social and instructional purposes within the school setting.

- **Standard 2:** English language learners communicate information, ideas and concepts necessary for academic success in the content area of language arts.

# About the Author—Homer

Little is known with any certainty about Homer, who is credited with having written or composed the ancient Greek epic poem *The Odyssey* and its companion epic, *The Iliad*. Although we read these works today in the way we might read a novel, originally these were works intended to be sung or recited in a performance setting. Tradition has it that Homer was himself a blind bard, but there is no real proof of this. The ancient Greek historian Herodotus (484–425 BCE) believed that Homer lived during the 800s BCE. However, most scholars today believe that *The Odyssey* was composed during the 700s BCE. Whatever the date of the poem's composition, tales of its hero, Odysseus, had almost certainly been in circulation for centuries by this time. In *The Odyssey*, Odysseus struggles to return home from the Trojan War, a war which archaeologists believe may have taken place around 1180 BCE. Stories about Odysseus and the other Trojan War heroes thus may have been passed down orally for three or four hundred years before Homer crafted *The Odyssey*.

# About the Translator—Robert Fagles

Robert Fagles was born in Philadelphia, Pennsylvania, in 1933. He attended Amherst College and received his doctorate from Yale University. He became an instructor of English and comparative literature at Princeton University in 1960. He was a popular teacher at Princeton and eventually became a full professor and head of the comparative literature department. In addition to translating *The Odyssey* into English, Fagles translated many other ancient Greek works, including the poetry of Bacchylides, plays by Aeschylus and Sophocles, and Homer's *The Iliad*. Fagles also translated Virgil's epic poem *The Aeneid* from Latin into English and was the author of a volume of his own poetry titled *I, Vincent: Poems from the Pictures of Van Gogh*. He received the National Book Award in Translation for his translation of *The Iliad* and the Academy Award in Literature from the American Academy of Arts and Letters for his translation of *The Odyssey*. Fagles was married and the father of two daughters. He died in 2008.

# Possible Texts for Text Comparisons

The lyric poems "The Lotos-Eaters" and "Ulysses" by Alfred Lord Tennyson are based on *The Odyssey* and can be taught in tandem with the epic. Both poems present story events from alternative perspectives.

The song "Calypso" by the folk-pop singer Suzanne Vega is a dramatic monologue in the voice of Calypso, one of *The Odyssey*'s female characters.

Modern novels based on *The Odyssey* include Zachary Mason's *The Lost Books of the Odyssey* (Picador, 2011) and Tracy Barrett's *King of Ithaka* (Henry Holt, 2010). Individual chapters of *The Lost Books of the Odyssey* work as short stories and may be taught as such.

# Cross-Curricular Connection

This book could be used during a history unit on ancient Greece or ancient cultures. It could also be paired with a study of ancient Greek or classical art.

# Book Summary of *The Odyssey*

Odysseus, the king of the Greek island of Ithaca, has been away from home for twenty years. He left his wife and baby son to cross the sea and fight in the Trojan War. After the war ended, Odysseus set out for home with a crew of men. However, disaster after disaster befell Odysseus, who had angered the powerful ocean god, Poseidon. Monsters and giants killed members of his crew. Other crew members died in a shipwreck. Now, only Odysseus remains alive, stranded on the island of the nymph Calypso, who wishes to keep him as her husband. Odysseus is miserable and homesick. Encouraged by the gods, Calypso agrees to let him go and sends him on his way on a raft. Poseidon wrecks the raft, but Odysseus manages to swim to shore, and he finds himself in the land of the friendly Phaeacians, who offer to ferry him home to Ithaca.

Meanwhile in Ithaca, Odysseus's faithful wife, Penelope, is still waiting for her husband to return. She does not wish to marry any of the many suitors who are occupying her house. She feels unable to send the arrogant and unmannered suitors away, but she continues to stall in selecting one of them as her husband.

Odysseus's son, Telemachus, is now a young man. He, too, feels angry with the suitors and wonders what has become of Odysseus. Inspired by the goddess Athena, Telemachus undertakes a sea voyage to visit two kings who fought alongside Odysseus in the Trojan War in hopes that one of them might have news of his father. While Telemachus is gone, the suitors plot to ambush his returning ship and kill him. However, Telemachus returns safely to Ithaca after learning that his father is still alive. Instead of going back to the palace, Telemachus visits the hut of the swineherd Eumaeus, a long time, faithful servant of the family. Eumaeus has another visitor, a storytelling beggar who Telemachus learns is his father in disguise. After a joyful, tearful reunion, father and son begin plotting the downfall of the suitors.

Odysseus, Eumaeus, and Telemachus journey to the palace. There, still in beggar costume, Odysseus begs for food from the suitors, who abuse and threaten him. He does not immediately retaliate, nor reveal his identity to Penelope, who has come up with a test by which she will select her future husband. She promises that she will marry whoever can string Odysseus's great bow and shoot an arrow through a row of axes. None of the suitors prove able to accomplish this feat, but Odysseus accomplishes the task easily. Bow in hand, he finally announces his identity and begins to shoot the suitors. With help from the goddess Athena, Odysseus, Telemachus, and Eumaeus are able to kill the suitors. After the fighting ends, Odysseus is joyfully reunited with Penelope as well as his father, Laertes. Although members of the suitors' families band together to avenge the suitors' deaths, Athena intervenes and brings peace.

## Possible Texts for Text Sets

- Marshall Cavendish Corp. *Ancient Greece*. Marshall Cavendish Corporation, 2010.
- Pearson, Anne. *Ancient Greece*. DK Publishing, 2007.
- Powell, Anton. *Ancient Greece*. Facts on File, 2003.
- Wright, Anne. *Inside Ancient Greece: Art and Architecture*. Sharpe Focus, 2008.

Name _____

Date _____

# Pre-Reading Theme Thoughts

**Directions:** Read each of the statements in the first column. Decide if you agree or disagree with the statements. Record your opinion by marking an X in Agree or Disagree for each statement. Explain your choices in the fourth column. There are no right or wrong answers.

| Statement | Agree | Disagree | Explain Your Answer |
|---|---|---|---|
| There's no place like home. | | | |
| One of the most important lessons you can learn in life is how to have self-control. | | | |
| Revenge is sweet and sometimes deserved. | | | |
| A clever mind is at least as important as a strong body. | | | |

# Vocabulary Overview

Ten key words from this section are provided below with definitions and sentences about how the words are used in the book. Choose one of the vocabulary activity sheets (pages 15 or 16) for students to complete as they read this section. Monitor students as they work to ensure the definitions they have found are accurate and relate to the text. Finally, discuss these important vocabulary words with students. If you think these words or other words in the section warrant more time devoted to them, there are suggestions in the introduction for other vocabulary activities (page 5).

| Word | Definition | Sentence about Text |
|---|---|---|
| harangue (Book 1) | to lecture someone in an aggressive and critical way | Zeus **harangues** the other gods on the subject of human misery. |
| distaff (Book 1) | a stick or spindle onto which wool is wound for spinning | A **distaff** and a loom are cloth-making tools that Penelope uses. |
| overweening (Book 1) | overly confident or proud | The suitors are **overweening** in their speech and behavior. |
| shroud (Book 2) | a wrap used to cover a dead person's body | Penelope spends three years weaving a **shroud** for Laertes. |
| portent (Book 2) | a sign that something important or terrible is about to happen | The seer views the actions of birds as a **portent**. |
| pernicious (Book 2) | harming in a slow, gradual way | Telemachus calls the suitors **pernicious** bullies. |
| libations (Book 2) | drinks that are poured out as offerings for gods | Telemachus pours **libations** to the gods so that they might grant him a safe journey. |
| hospitality (Book 4) | the friendly and generous reception of guests | Menelaus shows Telemachus **hospitality** when he arrives in Lacedaemon. |
| vaunt (Book 4) | a boast | The gods often respond to a **vaunt** by sending disaster to the braggart. |
| circumspect (Book 4) | thinking carefully about risks before acting | Penelope can be described as a person who is **circumspect**. |

# Understanding Vocabulary Words

**Directions:** The following words appear in this section of the book. Use context clues and reference materials to determine an accurate definition for each word.

| Word | Definition |
|---|---|
| harangue (Book 1) | |
| distaff (Book 1) | |
| overweening (Book 1) | |
| shroud (Book 2) | |
| portent (Book 2) | |
| pernicious (Book 2) | |
| libations (Book 2) | |
| hospitality (Book 4) | |
| vaunt (Book 4) | |
| circumspect (Book 4) | |

Name _____

Date _____

# During-Reading Vocabulary Activity

**Directions:** As you read these chapters, record at least eight important words on the lines below. Try to find interesting, difficult, intriguing, special, or funny words. Your words can be long or short. They can be hard or easy to spell. After each word, use context clues in the text and reference materials to define the word.

- _____
- _____
- _____
- _____
- _____
- _____
- _____
- _____
- _____
- _____

**Directions:** Respond to these questions about the words in this section.

1. In Book 2, what activity of the birds does Halitherses interpret as a **portent**, and what does he think it means?

_____

_____

2. What is something Nestor or Menelaus does to show **hospitality** to Telemachus?

_____

_____

# Analyzing the Literature

Provided below are discussion questions you can use in small groups, with the whole class, or for written assignments. Each question is given at two levels so you can choose the right question for each group of students. Activity sheets with these questions are provided (pages 18–19) if you want students to write their responses. For each question, a few key discussion points are provided for your reference.

| Story Element | ■ Level 1 | ▲ Level 2 | Key Discussion Points |
|---|---|---|---|
| Character | Who is Telemachus, and what are his feelings about the suitors? | How does Telemachus's behavior, especially toward his mother and the suitors, show that he is changing from a boy into a man? | Telemachus wishes to take control of his family's estates and is frustrated with the activities of the suitors. In Book 1, lines 409–439, he speaks out boldly to the suitors. In Book 2, he calls an assembly and then sets out on a voyage to discover the fate of his father. These behaviors show his change from boy to man. |
| Setting | Describe life at the palace in Ithaca. Who lives there, and what is happening there? | Compare and contrast life at the palace in Ithaca (Book 1) with life at Menelaus's palace in Sparta (Book 4). | Telemachus, his mother Penelope, their servants, and a gang of feasting, gaming suitors live at the palace in Ithaca. At Menelaus's palace, feasting also takes place, but the king is not absent and the environment is harmonious. The king and queen are clearly in control. |
| Character | Why do you think Penelope keeps putting off the decision to get remarried? How does she put it off? | What can we tell about Penelope from the way she tricks the suitors with her weaving project? | Penelope's deception with the shroud is first described in Book 2, lines 90–122. Penelope is clearly a skilled craftswoman and also very clever. We see that she is a good match for her clever husband. Her actions also show devotion to her husband's father, Laertes. |
| Plot | What are some ways that Athena helps Telemachus? | How important is the relationship of the gods to human beings in *The Odyssey*, and will it affect the outcome? | Athena takes a very active role in helping Telemachus. She fires him up so that he speaks out, prompts him to make his voyage, and assembles a crew for him. The gods interact directly with humans throughout *The Odyssey* and will have a large impact on the course of events. |

Name _____

Date _____

# Analyzing the Literature

**Directions:** Think about the section you just read. Read each question and state your response with textual evidence.

**1.** Who is Telemachus, and what are his feelings about the suitors?

_____

_____

_____

_____

**2.** Describe life at the palace in Ithaca. Who lives there, and what is happening there?

_____

_____

_____

_____

**3.** Why do you think Penelope keeps putting off the decision to get remarried? How does she put it off?

_____

_____

_____

_____

**4.** What are some ways that Athena helps Telemachus?

_____

_____

_____

Name _____

Date _____

# ▲ Analyzing the Literature

**Directions:** Think about the section you just read. Read each question and state your response with textual evidence.

1. How does Telemachus's behavior, especially toward his mother and the suitors, show that he is changing from a boy into a man?

_____

_____

_____

_____

2. Compare and contrast life at the palace in Ithaca (Book 1) with life at Menelaus's palace in Sparta (Book 4).

_____

_____

_____

_____

3. What can we tell about Penelope from the way she tricks the suitors with her weaving project?

_____

_____

_____

4. How important is the relationship of the gods to human beings in *The Odyssey*, and will it affect the outcome?

_____

_____

_____

Name _____

Date _____

# Reader Response

**Directions:** Choose one of the following prompts about this section to answer. Be sure you include a topic sentence in your response, use textual evidence to support your opinion, and provide a strong conclusion that summarizes your opinion.

## Writing Prompts

- **Argument Piece**—What is Zeus's view of human suffering, as stated in the opening of *The Odyssey*? Do you agree with Zeus? Give examples both from the story and from your own life to support your opinion.
- **Informative/Explanatory Piece**—The gods in Book 1, King Nestor in Book 3, and King Menelaus in Book 4 all discuss the fate of Agamemnon at the hands of his unfaithful wife, Clytemnestra. What happened to Agamemnon? How are Clytemnestra and Penelope similar, and how are they different?

_____

_____

_____

_____

_____

_____

_____

_____

_____

_____

_____

_____

# Close Reading the Literature

**Directions:** Closely reread Book 1, lines 112–206. Read each question, and then revisit the text to find evidence that supports your answer.

1. Locate the lines in the text where the suitors are introduced. What are they doing when we first meet them?

   _____

   _____

   _____

2. Think about what Telemachus is daydreaming about when we first meet him. What can we conclude about him based on this passage in the text?

   _____

   _____

   _____

3. The proper treatment of guests and strangers is a theme throughout *The Odyssey*. Use the text to point out specific things Telemachus does to properly welcome Athena when she arrives disguised as Mentes.

   _____

   _____

   _____

4. What kind of people do the suitors seem to be? Use evidence to describe how you know this.

   _____

   _____

   _____

Name _____

Date _____

# Making Connections–Ancient Technology

Below is a list of tools and other functional objects that are mentioned in the first four books of *The Odyssey*.

- chariot
- distaff
- loom
- lyre

- mixing-bowl
- set of smith's tools— hammer, anvil, and tongs
- ship

- spindle
- storage skins
- tripod

**Directions:** Select one object from the list. Use the library or Internet to research what this object might have looked like in Homeric times (800s–700s BCE) and how it functioned. Draw or print a picture of the object, or create a model of it. Find answers to the following questions about your selected object, and be ready to present this information to the class.

1. What was this object (or set of objects) used for?

2. How did it work?

3. How often do you think this object would have been used?

4. Who would have used it? Men, women, or both? The wealthy, the poor, or both?

5. Who uses the object in *The Odyssey*?

6. Is this same object, or a similar one, still in use today?

7. If it is still used today, how does today's version differ?

Name _____

Date _____

# Creating with the Story Elements

**Directions:** Thinking about the story elements of character, setting, and plot in a novel is very important to understanding what is happening and why. Complete **one** of the following activities based on what you've read so far. Be creative and have fun!

## Characters

Create a set of at least five "Character Profile Cards" for some or all of the characters from the first four books of *The Odyssey*. Include the following on each of the cards: *Physical Appearance*, *Age*, *Place of Residence*, *Strengths*, and *Weaknesses*. Use the text to help you fill in the profile information. Include an illustration of each character on the back of his or her card.

## Setting

Create a map that shows the route of Telemachus's voyage. For each location, include symbols on the map that provide information about the landscape, its inhabitants, and the livestock and crops. Also include a key. Find examples in the first four books of *The Odyssey*.

## Plot

Telemachus is very secretive about his travels to Lacedaemon (Sparta) and Pylos. What if this were not the case? What if he decided to write home about his trip? Whom might Telemachus write to? What might he say? Create two imaginary letters or postcards from Telemachus, one written during his visit to Pylos and the other during his visit to Lacedaemon.

# Vocabulary Overview

Ten key words from this section are provided below with definitions and sentences about how the words are used in the book. Choose one of the vocabulary activity sheets (pages 25 or 26) for students to complete as they read this section. Monitor students as they work to ensure the definitions they have found are accurate and relate to the text. Finally, discuss these important vocabulary words with students. If you think these words or other words in the section warrant more time devoted to them, there are suggestions in the introduction for other vocabulary activities (page 5).

| Word | Definition | Sentence about Text |
|------|-----------|---------------------|
| nymph (Book 5) | a divine being or nature spirit who takes the form of a beautiful woman | Calypso is described both as a **nymph** and as a goddess. |
| ambrosia (Book 5) | the food eaten by the gods in Greek mythology | The gods feast on **ambrosia** as they discuss Odysseus's fate. |
| lustrous (Book 5) | shining; glossy | Calypso is referred to as "the **lustrous** one." |
| suppliant (Book 6) | a person humbly asking for help from another person | Odysseus is a **suppliant** seeking help from the Phaeacians. |
| hallowed (Book 6) | sacred; holy | The grove of poplar trees sacred to Athena is **hallowed** ground. |
| convoy (Book 7) | a group of people, ships, or vehicles traveling together to protect and escort someone | Odysseus asks the Phaeacians to give him a rapid **convoy** home. |
| provisions (Book 7) | food, drink, and equipment needed for a journey | Calypso gives Odysseus **provisions** to take on the raft with him. |
| Muse (Book 8) | a goddess who inspires artists such as musicians and poets | The Phaeacians' bard, Demodocus, is described as inspired by the **Muse**. |
| oracle (Book 8) | a priest or priestess who makes a prophecy or gives advice | One might consult an **oracle** to find out about the future, as Agamemnon does in Demodocus's song. |
| bellwether (Book 9) | the leader of a flock of sheep | Odysseus hides under the **bellwether** in his escape from the Cyclops's cave. |

Name _____

Date _____

# Understanding Vocabulary Words

**Directions:** The following words appear in this section of the book. Use context clues and reference materials to determine an accurate definition for each word.

| Word | Definition |
|---|---|
| nymph (Book 5) | |
| ambrosia (Book 5) | |
| lustrous (Book 5) | |
| suppliant (Book 6) | |
| hallowed (Book 6) | |
| convoy (Book 7) | |
| provisions (Book 7) | |
| Muse (Book 8) | |
| oracle (Book 8) | |
| bellwether (Book 9) | |

Name _____

Date _____

# During-Reading Vocabulary Activity

**Directions:** As you read these chapters, record at least eight important words on the lines below. Try to find interesting, difficult, intriguing, special, or funny words. Your words can be long or short. They can be hard or easy to spell. After each word, use context clues in the text and reference materials to define the word.

- _____
- _____
- _____
- _____
- _____
- _____
- _____
- _____
- _____
- _____

**Directions:** Respond to these questions about the words in this section.

1. Which character is a **nymph**, and how is she different from an ordinary person?

_____

_____

2. From whom does Odysseus request a **convoy**, and why does he need one?

_____

_____

# Analyzing the Literature

Provided below are discussion questions you can use in small groups, with the whole class, or for written assignments. Each question is given at two levels so you can choose the right question for each group of students. Activity sheets with these questions are provided (pages 28–29) if you want students to write their responses. For each question, a few key discussion points are provided for your reference.

| Story Element | ■ Level 1 | ▲ Level 2 | Key Discussion Points |
|---|---|---|---|
| Character | What is Odysseus doing when we finally meet him in Book 5? | What benefits would Odysseus gain from staying with Calypso? What can we tell about Odysseus and his values from his desire to leave her? | We meet Odysseus in person in Book 5, line 92. He is gazing out to sea and crying. Despite having a beautiful lover, an easy life, and the promise of immortality, Odysseus wants nothing more than to return to his wife, family, and homeland. |
| Character | Do you think it is fair to say that Odysseus has been a prisoner on Calypso's island? Why or why not? | Could/should Odysseus have left Calypso's island sooner, and has he been faithful to Penelope? | Odysseus could have left the island earlier if he wished, as the materials to make the raft were there. Odysseus has not been physically faithful to Penelope. Students may argue that he has been faithful psychologically, however. |
| Plot | Name some female characters that help Odysseus in Books 5–9. Who helps him the most? | At this point, would you say that the female characters are more often helpful or harmful? Are they powerful or without power? | A number of female characters, including Calypso, Ino, Athena, Nausicaa, and Arete all help Odysseus in Books 5–9. These characters either have supernatural powers or are able to use their social positions to help Odysseus. Students can compare and contrast these characters with Penelope and Eurycleia, introduced in Books 1–4. |
| Setting | Describe the first two places Odysseus travels after leaving Troy. How do the crew members lose their self-control in both places? | Describe the first two places Odysseus travels after leaving Troy. What weaknesses do the crew show, and what lessons are learned from these episodes? | The men visited the land of the Cicones first, where they sack a city, steal goods, and take women captive. The crew members are unwilling to stop their partying and leave when told to do so. The crew also loses control of themselves on the Lotus-eaters' isle by eating of the lotus and losing the desire to return home. |

Name _____

Date _____

# Analyzing the Literature

**Directions:** Think about the section you just read. Read each question and state your response with textual evidence.

1. What is Odysseus doing when we finally meet him in Book 5?

_____

_____

_____

_____

2. Do you think it is fair to say that Odysseus has been a prisoner on Calypso's island? Why or why not?

_____

_____

_____

_____

3. Name some female characters that help Odysseus in Books 5–9. Who helps him the most?

_____

_____

_____

_____

4. Describe the first two places Odysseus travels with his crew after leaving Troy. How do the crew members lose their self-control in both places?

_____

_____

_____

Name _____

Date _____

# ▲ Analyzing the Literature

**Directions:** Think about the section you just read.  Read each question and state your response with textual evidence.

1. What benefits would Odysseus gain from staying with Calypso?  What can we tell about Odysseus and his values from his desire to leave her?

_____

_____

_____

_____

2. Could/should Odysseus have left Calypso's island sooner, and has he been faithful to Penelope?

_____

_____

_____

_____

3. At this point, would you say that female characters in *The Odyssey* are more often helpful or harmful?  Are they powerful or without power?

_____

_____

_____

4. Describe the first two places Odysseus travels after leaving Troy.  What weaknesses do the crew show, and what lessons are learned from these episodes?

_____

_____

_____

Name _____

Date _____

# Reader Response

**Directions:** Choose one of the following prompts about this section to answer. Be sure you include a topic sentence in your response, use textual evidence to support your opinion, and provide a strong conclusion that summarizes your opinion.

## Writing Prompts

- **Informational/Explanatory Piece**—How are strangers and suppliants supposed to be treated, according to Homer's epic? Do you think your own culture takes a similar view of how a stranger in need ought to be treated? Describe an event from your own life or culture to support your answer.

- **Argument Piece**—During the Phaeacian games (Book 8), Odysseus talks about how important it is to have "winning self-control" (line 198). Argue that Odysseus has such self-control, lacks self-control, or is learning to have self-control. Give examples from *The Odyssey* to support your answer.

_____

_____

_____

_____

_____

_____

_____

_____

_____

_____

_____

_____

Name _____

Date _____

# Close Reading the Literature

**Directions:** Closely reread Odysseus's story about escaping the Cyclops in Book 9, lines 443–595. Read each question and then revisit the text to find evidence that supports your answer.

1. Locate the passage in the text where Odysseus describes Polyphemus calling out to his neighbors for help. Why don't the neighbors come?

   _____

   _____

2. Locate the passage describing how Odysseus and his men get out of the cave without the Cyclops detecting them. How do they escape, and what positive qualities or talents does Odysseus exhibit here?

   _____

   _____

   _____

3. How does Odysseus behave as he and his men sail away from the land of the Cyclops? What do his men seem to think of this behavior? Cite evidence from the text to support your conclusion.

   _____

   _____

   _____

4. Why was it a huge mistake for Odysseus to reveal his real name to the Cyclops? Why do you think he does it? Use the text to support your claim.

   _____

   _____

   _____

Name _____

Date _____

# Making Connections–Epic Similes

**Directions:** *The Odyssey* is full of extended similes, sometimes called *epic similes*. These long comparisons help readers better understand the characters' emotions and visualize the action. Locate the following extended similes and metaphors in Books 5–9 of *The Odyssey*. Write the two things that are being compared.

| Simile/Metaphor | Comparison 1 | Comparison 2 |
|---|---|---|
| Book 5, lines 436–442 | | |
| Book 5, lines 472–478 | | |
| Book 5, lines 540–547 | | |
| Book 6, lines 112–121 | | |
| Book 7, lines 139–148 | | |
| Book 7, lines 251–256 | | |
| Book 8, lines 585–597 | | |
| Book 9, lines 429–441 | | |

# Creating with the Story Elements

**Directions:** Thinking about the story elements of character, setting, and plot in a novel is very important to understanding what is happening and why. Complete **one** of the following activities based on what you've read so far. Be creative and have fun!

## Characters

Create a set of at least five "Character Profile Cards" for some or all of the characters from Books 5–9, using the text to provide profile information. Include the following on each of the cards: *Physical Appearance*, *Age*, *Place of Residence*, *Strengths*, and *Weaknesses*.

## Setting

Create a travel brochure for one of the locations described in Books 5–9. Include a detailed description of the location, climate, potential recreation activities, places to visit, and local cuisine. Include illustrations, photos, and/or a map.

## Plot

Create a sporting event program for the Phaeacian games that take place in Book 8. Include a schedule of events, descriptions of the events, and information about the athletes. Include illustrations and photos. Add additional sporting event program elements such as scorecards.

# Vocabulary Overview

Ten key words from this section are provided below with definitions and sentences about how the words are used in the book. Choose one of the vocabulary activity sheets (pages 35 or 36) for students to complete as they read this section. Monitor students as they work to ensure the definitions they have found are accurate and relate to the text. Finally, discuss these important vocabulary words with students. If you think these words or other words in the section warrant more time devoted to them, there are suggestions in the introduction for other vocabulary activities (page 5).

| Word | Definition | Sentence about Text |
|---|---|---|
| ramparts (Book 10) | defensive walls topped with walkways | Aeolus's island is ringed with **ramparts**. |
| sumptuous (Book 10) | splendid; expensive looking | The Laestrygonian king lives in a **sumptuous** palace. |
| shades (Book 11) | disembodied spirits; ghosts | In Hades, Odysseus meets the **shades** of the dead. |
| campaigner (Book 11) | someone who has worked with others to bring about a result, as in a military campaign | Odysseus is sometimes called a **campaigner** since he led troops during the Trojan War. |
| intrepid (Book 11) | feeling no fear | Odysseus describes the famous heroes Castor and Pollux as **intrepid**. |
| cortege (Book 11) | a line of people; a procession | A **cortege** of spirits appears before Odysseus when he is in Hades. |
| baldric (Book 11) | an ornamented belt worn over the shoulder to support a sword | Odysseus seems amazed by the fancy **baldric** worn by the hero Heracles. |
| beetling (Book 12) | prominent or overhanging | Circe warns Odysseus to avoid **beetling** cliffs called the Clashing Rocks. |
| riven (Book 12) | violently torn apart | Several of Odysseus's men are **riven** by the monster Scylla. |
| upbraid (Book 12) | to scold or find fault with | Odysseus **upbraids** his men for killing the cattle of the Sun. |

# Understanding Vocabulary Words

**Directions:** The following words appear in this section of the book. Use context clues and reference materials to determine an accurate definition for each word.

| Word | Definition |
|------|------------|
| ramparts (Book 10) | |
| sumptuous (Book 10) | |
| shades (Book 11) | |
| campaigner (Book 11) | |
| intrepid (Book 11) | |
| cortege (Book 11) | |
| baldric (Book 11) | |
| beetling (Book 12) | |
| riven (Book 12) | |
| upbraid (Book 12) | |

Name _____

Date _____

# During-Reading Vocabulary Activity

**Directions:** As you read these chapters, record at least eight important words on the lines below. Try to find interesting, difficult, intriguing, special, or funny words. Your words can be long or short. They can be hard or easy to spell. After each word, use context clues in the text and reference materials to define the word.

- _____
- _____
- _____
- _____
- _____
- _____
- _____
- _____
- _____
- _____

**Directions:** Now, organize your words. Rewrite each of the words on a sticky note. Work with a group to create a bar graph of your words. Stack any words that are the same on top of one another. Different words should appear in different columns. Finally, discuss with the group why certain words were chosen more often than other words.

# Analyzing the Literature

Provided below are discussion questions you can use in small groups, with the whole class, or for written assignments. Each question is given at two levels so you can choose the right question for each group of students. Activity sheets with these questions are provided (pages 38–39) if you want students to write their responses. For each question, a few key discussion points are provided for your reference.

| Story Element | ■ Level 1 | ▲ Level 2 | Key Discussion Points |
|---|---|---|---|
| Setting | In *The Odyssey*, is the Kingdom of the Dead a good place, a bad place, or neither? Explain your answer. | What view of the afterlife do we see in *The Odyssey*? What connection might Tantalus and Sisyphus have to Odysseus? | In Book 11, lines 547–558, Achilles says he would rather be a living slave than a dead hero. Tantalus is tormented by food he cannot eat, just as Odysseus and his crew will be on the Island of Helios. Sisyphus's labor seems related to the way in which Odysseus keeps circling back and repeating parts of his voyage. |
| Character | Who does Agamemnon's ghost advise Odysseus to be wary of? Do you think he should follow this advice? | What advice does Odysseus get from Agamemnon's ghost? What does he do in Ithaca that shows he plans to pay attention to that advice? | Agamemnon's ghost cautions Odysseus to be careful, hide his identity, and not to readily trust Penelope or others (Book 11, lines 499–518). Odysseus shows caution and self-control back on Ithaca when he lies about his identity and hides his gifts. |
| Plot | Point out some places in *The Odyssey* where food or eating is mentioned. Are you surprised at how often food/eating comes up in the story? Why or why not? | Talk about the role that food and hunger play in *The Odyssey*. So far, how has the course of events been affected by food or hunger? | *The Odyssey* has been jokingly called "the eatingest epic." In the story, eating binds characters together and creates friendships. However, eating what has not been willingly given, due to hunger or greed, results in conflict and disaster, as is seen with the cattle of Helios. |
| Setting | How do trees help, protect, or support Odysseus in *The Odyssey*? | Where are some places in which trees are mentioned? Are trees more often helpful or harmful? Threatening or protective? | Trees play a supportive and protective role. Olive trees, viewed by the Greeks as a gift from Athena, hide Odysseus on Phaeacia and greet him when he returns to Ithaca. Earlier, a stake made from an olive tree saved Odysseus from the Cyclops. A fig tree saved him from Charybdis. |

Name _____

Date _____

# ■ Analyzing the Literature

**Directions:** Think about the section you just read. Read each question and state your response with textual evidence.

1. In *The Odyssey*, is the Kingdom of the Dead a good place, a bad place, or neither? Explain your answer.

_____

_____

_____

_____

2. Who does Agamemnon's ghost advise Odysseus to be wary of? Do you think he should follow this advice?

_____

_____

_____

_____

3. Point out some places in *The Odyssey* where food or eating is mentioned. Are you surprised at how often food/eating comes up in the story? Why or why not?

_____

_____

_____

4. How do trees help, protect, or support Odysseus in *The Odyssey*?

_____

_____

_____

## ▲ Analyzing the Literature

**Directions:** Think about the section you just read. Read each question and state your response with textual evidence.

1. What view of the afterlife do we see in *The Odyssey*? What connection might Tantalus and Sisyphus have to Odysseus?

_____

_____

_____

_____

2. What advice does Odysseus get from Agamemnon's ghost? What does he do in Ithaca that shows he plans to pay attention to that advice?

_____

_____

_____

_____

3. Talk about the role that food and hunger play in *The Odyssey*. So far, how has the course of events been affected by food or hunger?

_____

_____

_____

4. Where are some places in which trees are mentioned? Are trees more often helpful or harmful? Threatening or protective?

_____

_____

_____

Name _____

Date _____

# Reader Response

**Directions:** Choose one of the following prompts about this section to answer. Be sure you include a topic sentence in your response, use textual evidence to support your opinion, and provide a strong conclusion that summarizes your opinion.

## Writing Prompts

- **Argument Piece**—Odysseus can choose who he wishes to speak with in Hades, and he speaks with many different spirits. If you could journey to the land of the dead like Odysseus, to whom would you choose to speak and why?

- **Narrative Piece**—Odysseus tells the Phaeacians the story of his adventures in Books 9–12. We hear about what happened from his point of view. Select one of the episodes from his long story and retell it from the point of view of another character. For instance, describe the meeting with Circe from her point of view or from the point of view of one of the crew members turned to swine.

_____

_____

_____

_____

_____

_____

_____

_____

_____

_____

_____

_____

_____

Name _____

Date _____

# Close Reading the Literature

**Directions:** Closely reread the passage in which Odysseus visits Eumaeus in disguise in Book 14, lines 26–110. Read each question, and then revisit the text to find evidence that supports your answer.

1. What can we tell about Odysseus and Eumaeus from how they act during Odysseus's encounter with the herding dogs? Use the text to support your claims.

   _____

   _____

   _____

2. Cite evidence to explain Eumaeus's feelings about his old master, Odysseus.

   _____

   _____

   _____

3. What does Eumaeus think about the suitors?

   _____

   _____

   _____

4. How and why does Eumaeus show hospitality to Odysseus in his beggar's disguise? Support your answer with references from the text.

   _____

   _____

   _____

   _____

Name _____ _____

Date _____

# Making Connections–Characters and Epithets

**Directions:** An *epithet* is an adjective or descriptive phrase that expresses a quality or a characteristic of something or someone. In Homer's *The Odyssey*, characters' names are frequently paired with epithets. For instance, Circe is introduced as "Circe, the nymph with lovely braids." Who is being described in each of the epithets below?

1. Young _____ , with her rose-red fingers (*Book 10, line 205*)

2. _____ , god of the golden wand (*Book 10, line 305*)

3. Royal son of Laertes, _____ , tried and true (*Book 10, line 443*)

4. _____ , majesty, shining among your island people (*Book 11, line 404*)

5. _____ , son of Peleus, greatest of the Achaeans (*Book 11, line 542*)

6. _____ , ghoul of the cliffs (*Book 12, line 250*)

7. _____ , the son of Cronus (*Book 12, line 437*)

8. _____ , master of the sea (*Book 13, line 212*)

9. _____ , daughter of storming Zeus (*Book 13, line 285*)

10. _____ , the godlike boy (*Book 14, line 200*)

**Bonus:** Invent some of your own Homeric epithets to describe your friends and family members.

# Creating with the Story Elements

**Directions:** Thinking about the story elements of character, setting, and plot in a novel is very important to understanding what is happening and why. Complete **one** of the following activities based on what you've read so far. Be creative and have fun!

## Characters

Pretend you are a talk show host. Odysseus or another character from *The Odyssey* is about to appear on your show. Create questions that you would like to ask this character. How might the character respond? Write a script for the show, or perform the interview with a friend.

## Setting

Create a collage representing Odysseus's thoughts and feelings about Ithaca. Include images related to objects, people, and situations that he has already encountered there as well as objects, people, and situations that he is likely to encounter. Be ready to explain your inclusion of each element of your collage.

## Plot

On a poster or using a computer program, create a flowchart that maps out Odysseus's movement from Troy back home to Ithaca. Use different shapes and colors to represent different types of places Odysseus stops and/or the different types of obstacles he faces along the way. Use arrows of one color to signify forward motion and arrows of another color to signify places where he doubles back. Include a key.

# Vocabulary Overview

Ten key words from this section are provided below with definitions and sentences about how the words are used in the book. Choose one of the vocabulary activity sheets (pages 45 or 46) for students to complete as they read this section. Monitor students as they work to ensure the definitions they have found are accurate and relate to the text. Finally, discuss these important vocabulary words with students. If you think these words or other words in the section warrant more time devoted to them, there are suggestions in the introduction for other vocabulary activities (page 5).

| Word | Definition | Sentence about Text |
|---|---|---|
| irreproachable (Book 15) | faultless; beyond criticism | Penelope's behavior is sometimes described as **irreproachable**. |
| insolence (Book 16) | rude and disrespectful behavior | The suitors often display **insolence**, and they also accuse Telemachus of it. |
| patrimony (Book 16) | property inherited from a father | Telemachus is concerned about the loss of his **patrimony**. |
| disabuse (Book 16) | to persuade someone that they have an incorrect frame of mind | The suitors urge Penelope to **disabuse** herself of her worries over Telemachus. |
| cadge (Book 17) | to ask for something to which one is not entitled | The suitors are annoyed that a beggar in their midst is about to **cadge** a meal. |
| debauched (Book 17) | overindulging in things that bring sensual pleasure | The **debauched** suitors eat, drink, and play all day. |
| vagrant (Book 17) | a person without a settled home who wanders from place to place | Athena disguises Odysseus as a **vagrant** beggar. |
| unguent (Book 18) | a lotion or an ointment | Athena rubs a divine **unguent** on Penelope's skin to restore its beauty. |
| demur (Book 19) | to object or voice opposition | Penelope **demurs** when others comment on her beauty. |
| evanescent (Book 19) | quickly fading or disappearing | Penelope describes the two gateways through which **evanescent** dreams come during sleep. |

Name _____

Date _____

# Understanding Vocabulary Words

**Directions:** The following words appear in this section of the book. Use context clues and reference materials to determine an accurate definition for each word.

| Word | Definition |
|---|---|
| irreproachable (Book 15) | |
| insolence (Book 16) | |
| patrimony (Book 16) | |
| disabuse (Book 16) | |
| cadge (Book 17) | |
| debauched (Book 17) | |
| vagrant (Book 17) | |
| unguent (Book 18) | |
| demur (Book 19) | |
| evanescent (Book 19) | |

Name _____

Date _____

# During-Reading Vocabulary Activity

**Directions:** As you read these chapters, record at least eight important words on the lines below. Try to find interesting, difficult, intriguing, special, or funny words. Your words can be long or short. They can be hard or easy to spell. After each word, use context clues in the text and reference materials to define the word.

- _____
- _____
- _____
- _____
- _____
- _____
- _____
- _____
- _____
- _____

**Directions:** Respond to these questions about the words in this section.

1. Why is Telemachus concerned about his **patrimony**?

_____

_____

2. What behaviors of the suitors reveal that they are **debauched**?

_____

_____

# Analyzing the Literature

Provided below are discussion questions you can use in small groups, with the whole class, or for written assignments. Each question is given at two levels so you can choose the right question for each group of students. Activity sheets with these questions are provided (pages 48–49) if you want students to write their responses. For each question, a few key discussion points are provided for your reference.

| Story Element | ■ Level 1 | ▲ Level 2 | Key Discussion Points |
|---|---|---|---|
| Plot | Describe the condition of Odysseus's dog, Argos, in Book 17. How do you think Odysseus feels seeing the dog in such condition? | How is Argos the dog symbolic of Odysseus's estate, his family, or his feelings about himself? | Odysseus's dog recognizes him in Book 17, lines 317–360. Argos's condition seems to mirror that of Odysseus's estate and of Odysseus himself, who returns older and dressed in beggar's rags. However, Argos has been waiting for his master all these years, so the dog's presence is a sign that the memory of Odysseus and hope for his return has remained alive in Ithaca. |
| Character | Do you think Odysseus should stand up for himself instead of taking abuse from the suitors? Why or why not? | Why do you think Odysseus tolerates and even provokes abuse from the suitors? What is he trying to achieve? | Odysseus seems to be testing the character of the suitors in Books 17–18. He is perhaps building up reasons to take them down and building up the anger and determination that will help him do so. |
| Setting/ Character | Penelope is sometimes described as sitting or standing in front of a pillar of the house. How is Penelope like a pillar of the house? | When Penelope appears downstairs, she stands in front of or leans against a pillar. What might this action/location symbolize? | Penelope has been "holding down the fort" for 20 years. She has been a "pillar of strength" in the face of adversity. Alternatively, the action of leaning against the pillar could also be interpreted as a need for support. In keeping her back to the pillar, Penelope might be "watching her back." |
| Plot | Do you think Odysseus should reveal his identity to Penelope sooner than he does? Why or why not? | Does Odysseus reveal his identity to Penelope in Book 19? Does she recognize him? If she knows it's him, why does she continue to act as if she doesn't? | Students will vary in their opinions about whether Odysseus should hold out in revealing his identity to Penelope. His description of the clothes (Book 19, lines 259–270) is so complete that in describing them, he may be revealing himself. Penelope slips when speaking to Eurycleia in lines 406–407, indicating that she knows, at least subconsciously, the identity of the beggar. |

Name _____

Date _____

## Analyzing the Literature

**Directions:** Think about the section you just read. Read each question and state your response with textual evidence.

1. Describe the condition of Odysseus's dog, Argos, encountered in Book 17. How do you think Odysseus feels, seeing the dog in such condition?

_____

_____

_____

_____

2. Do you think Odysseus should stand up for himself instead of taking abuse from the suitors? Why or why not?

_____

_____

_____

_____

3. Penelope is sometimes described as sitting or standing in front of a pillar of the house. How is Penelope like a pillar of the house?

_____

_____

_____

4. Do you think Odysseus should reveal his identity to Penelope sooner than he does? Why or why not?

_____

_____

_____

Name _____

Date _____

# ▲ Analyzing the Literature

**Directions:** Think about the section you just read. Read each question and state your response with textual evidence.

1. How is Argos the dog symbolic of Odysseus's estate, his family, or his feelings about himself?

_____

_____

_____

_____

2. Why do you think Odysseus tolerates and even provokes abuse from the suitors? What is he trying to achieve?

_____

_____

_____

_____

3. When Penelope appears downstairs, she stands in front of or leans against a pillar. What might this action/location symbolize?

_____

_____

_____

4. Does Odysseus reveal his identity to Penelope in Book 19? Does she recognize him? If she knows it's him, why does she continue to act as if she doesn't?

_____

_____

_____

Name _____

Date _____

# Reader Response

**Directions:** Choose one of the following prompts about this section to answer. Be sure you include a topic sentence in your response, use textual evidence to support your opinion, and provide a strong conclusion that summarizes your opinion.

## Writing Prompts

- **Argument Piece**—Compare and contrast Odysseus's scar and a scar of your own. Do you view your scar as a reminder of trauma? A badge of pride? An annoying imperfection? Argue that Odysseus would view his scar in a similar or different way.

- **Informative/Explanatory Piece**—Eumaeus explains how he experienced a quick and unexpected change of fortune when he was just a boy. What happened to Eumaeus? Describe some other places in *The Odyssey* where characters experience rapid and drastic changes of fortune.

_____

_____

_____

_____

_____

_____

_____

_____

_____

_____

_____

_____

_____

# Close Reading the Literature

**Directions:** Closely reread the passage in Book 19 where Eurycleia recognizes Odysseus, lines 443–538. Read each question, and then revisit the text to find evidence that supports your answer.

**1.** Use the text to describe how Eurycleia identifies Odysseus. What are her feelings about him?

_____

_____

_____

**2.** Based on the events mentioned in the epic tale, how did Odysseus get the scar on his leg?

_____

_____

_____

**3.** What was Odysseus like as a boy? What evidence in this passage helps you to draw this conclusion?

_____

_____

_____

**4.** Has Odysseus changed much since boyhood? Use textual evidence to support your opinion.

_____

_____

_____

Name _____

Date _____

# Making Connections–Wise Words T-Shirt

**Directions:** In these books of *The Odyssey*, Odysseus is dressed in rags. What if you could give him a new shirt? Select one of the inspirational slogans below to have printed on Odysseus's T-shirt. Then, explain on the lines below why you selected that particular slogan.

- *Obstacles are those frightful things you see when you take your eyes off the goal.—*Henry Ford

- Don't give up what you want most for what you want now.

- *I don't measure a man's success by how high he climbs, but by how high he bounces when he hits bottom.—*George S. Patton

- The loyalty of dogs proves that there is human potential.

- *Forgiveness is a virtue of the brave.—*Indira Gandhi

- Don't trust words. Trust actions.

- *Nobody can make you feel inferior without your consent.—*Eleanor Roosevelt

- Love is a journey starting at forever and ending at never.

Dear Odysseus,

Here is a new shirt for you to change into. I chose a shirt with this particular slogan on it because . . . .

_____

_____

_____

_____

_____

_____

_____

Name _____

Date _____

# Creating with the Story Elements

**Directions:** Thinking about the story elements of character, setting, and plot in a novel is very important to understanding what is happening and why. Complete **one** of the following activities based on what you've read so far. Be creative and have fun!

## Characters

Pretend you are a director about to cast a movie version of *The Odyssey*. What actors would you select to play the various characters? Why? Cast at least five characters for your movie by writing detailed explanations of why you have chosen the actors that you have chosen. You may wish to include photographs of the actors with your descriptions.

## Setting

Draw the interior of the palace at Ithaca where the action takes place in these and the following books. You may use an architectural or a cutaway style of drawing for this assignment. Label areas of the palace where various events take place. For example, you might write "This is the storage room where Telemachus locks the suitors' weapons."

## Plot

Without looking ahead in the book, write plot summaries for at least two possible endings for *The Odyssey*. Draw one or both of the endings in comic book or graphic novel form.

# Vocabulary Overview

Ten key words from this section are provided below with definitions and sentences about how the words are used in the book. Choose one of the vocabulary activity sheets (pages 55 or 56) for students to complete as they read this section. Monitor students as they work to ensure the definitions they have found are accurate and relate to the text. Finally, discuss these important vocabulary words with students. If you think these words or other words in the section warrant more time devoted to them, there are suggestions in the introduction for other vocabulary activities (page 5).

| Word | Definition | Sentence about Text |
|------|------------|---------------------|
| congenial (Book 20) | suitable or pleasing | Agelaus, one of the suitors, hopes that Telemachus finds his advice **congenial**. |
| charlatan (Book 20) | a person pretending to have more knowledge or skill than he or she has | The suitors call the seer Theoclymenus a **charlatan** after he describes his vision of their downfall. |
| tamp (Book 21) | to force something down with repeated light blows | Telemachus **tamps** the axes into the ground so that the suitors can attempt the test of the bow. |
| pique (Book 21) | a feeling of irritation | The suitors feel **pique** when Odysseus is given a chance to shoot the bow. |
| buckler (Book 22) | a round shield held by a grip | Odysseus uses a helmet and a **buckler** as protection when fighting the suitors. |
| salvo (Book 22) | a simultaneous discharge of weaponry | Odysseus and those fighting with him attack the suitors with a **salvo** of thrown spears. |
| stockade (Book 22) | a barrier of strong posts | The disloyal maidservants stand before the **stockade** when they have been forced out of the hall. |
| dirge (Book 24) | a mournful funeral song | Agamemnon remembers the **dirge** the Muses sang when Achilles died. |
| brusquely (Book 24) | in an abrupt manner | Odysseus speaks **brusquely** when questioned about Penelope. |
| droves (Book 24) | a large number of people or animals, usually in motion | The dead suitors reflect on how Odysseus was able to kill **droves** of them. |

Name _____

Date _____

# Understanding Vocabulary Words

**Directions:** The following words appear in this section of the book. Use context clues and reference materials to determine an accurate definition for each word.

| Word | Definition |
|---|---|
| congenial (Book 20) | |
| charlatan (Book 20) | |
| tamp (Book 21) | |
| pique (Book 21) | |
| buckler (Book 22) | |
| salvo (Book 22) | |
| stockade (Book 22) | |
| dirge (Book 24) | |
| brusquely (Book 24) | |
| droves (Book 24) | |

Name _____

Date _____

# During-Reading Vocabulary Activity

**Directions:** As you read these chapters, choose five important words from the story. Use these words to complete the word flow chart below. On each arrow, write a word. In each box, explain how the connected pair of words relates to each other. An example for the words *buckler* and *droves* has been done for you.

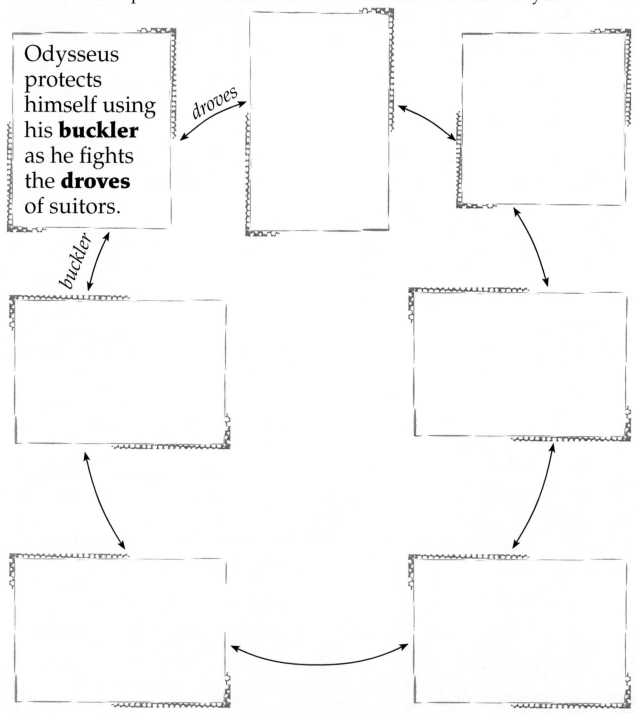

Odysseus protects himself using his **buckler** as he fights the **droves** of suitors.

*droves*

*buckler*

# Analyzing the Literature

Provided below are discussion questions you can use in small groups, with the whole class, or for written assignments. Each question is given at two levels so you can choose the right question for each group of students. Activity sheets with these questions are provided (pages 58–59) if you want students to write their responses. For each question, a few key discussion points are provided for your reference.

| Story Element | ■ Level 1 | ▲ Level 2 | Key Discussion Points |
|---|---|---|---|
| Character | Should Odysseus take the deal offered by Eurymachus in Book 22, lines 54–59? Why or why not? | Why doesn't Odysseus accept Eurymachus's deal (Book 22, lines 54–59)? If he did accept the deal, would that make for a better or worse ending of the story? | Eurymachus offers to pay back Odysseus and replenish his decimated livestock. Odysseus is very angry by this point from the treatment he has endured. He also may not trust the suitors. Students may argue that such a settlement would make for an anticlimactic ending. |
| Character | Is Odysseus's treatment of the "disloyal" maids too harsh? | What are the "disloyal" maids guilty of doing? Is their guilt equal to that of the suitors? | The maids who have been consorting with the suitors are also killed after being forced to clean the battle mess. Some students may feel that the maids are not as "guilty" as the suitors and that the expectation for them to remain chaste and loyal to a master they've never met has an element of sexism to it. |
| Setting | What role do trees play in the reunion scene between Odysseus and Laertes? | Where does Odysseus meet Laertes, and why is the location significant? What do trees seem to symbolize here? | Odysseus meets his father in the orchard. Odysseus proves his identity by pointing out trees that were childhood gifts from his father. The trees symbolize stability, strength, longevity, and unshakeable family ties. Students may note how a tree is also featured in the scene where Odysseus proves his identity to Penelope. |
| Plot | Why does Athena need to step in and stop the violence at the end of The Odyssey? | Athena brings peace at the end, but do you think Ithaca and Odysseus can continue to have a peaceful future after what Odysseus has done? Why or why not? | Athena needs to stop the cycle of revenge because in a revenge-oriented society, one killing will most likely lead to another unless someone intervenes and forces a resolution. Some students may think it unlikely that Odysseus will be trusted/loved/revered as a king after what he's done to the suitors. |

Name _____

Date _____

# Analyzing the Literature

**Directions:** Think about the section you just read. Read each question and state your response with textual evidence.

1. Should Odysseus take the deal offered by Eurymachus in Book 22, lines 54–59? Why or why not?

_____

_____

_____

_____

2. Is Odysseus's treatment of the "disloyal" maids too harsh?

_____

_____

_____

_____

3. What role do trees play in the reunion scene between Odysseus and Laertes?

_____

_____

_____

_____

4. Why does Athena need to step in and stop the violence at the end of *The Odyssey*?

_____

_____

_____

Name _____

Date _____

# ▲ Analyzing the Literature

**Directions:** Think about the section you just read. Read each question and state your response with textual evidence.

1. Why doesn't Odysseus accept Eurymachus's deal (Book 22, lines 54–59)? If he did accept the deal, would that make for a better or worse ending of the story?

_____

_____

_____

_____

2. What are the "disloyal" maids guilty of doing? Is their guilt equal to that of the suitors?

_____

_____

_____

_____

3. Where does Odysseus meet Laertes, and why is the location significant? What do trees seem to symbolize here?

_____

_____

_____

4. Athena brings peace at the end, but do you think Ithaca and Odysseus can continue to have a peaceful future after what Odysseus has done? Why or why not?

_____

_____

_____

Name _____

Date _____

# Reader Response

**Directions:** Choose one of the following prompts about this section to answer. Be sure you include a topic sentence in your response, use textual evidence to support your opinion, and provide a strong conclusion that summarizes your opinion.

## Writing Prompts

- **Informative/Explanatory Piece**—Focusing on evidence from the last five books of *The Odyssey*, think about what trees symbolize in *The Odyssey*. Then explain what they symbolize to you and to the culture in which you live. Point out how your own or your culture's view of trees seems similar to and/or different from that found in *The Odyssey*.
- **Narrative Piece**—Write an alternative ending to *The Odyssey* in which Odysseus pardons the suitors *or* Athena fails to step in and stop the battle with the suitors' families.

_____

_____

_____

_____

_____

_____

_____

_____

_____

_____

_____

_____

Name _____

Date _____

# Close Reading the Literature

**Directions:** Closely reread the passage where Odysseus and Penelope are finally reunited in Book 23, lines 186–271. Read each question, and then revisit the text to find evidence that supports your answer.

**1.** Using the text, explain what Penelope says to Eurycleia in order to test Odysseus one final time.

_____

_____

_____

**2.** What is unique about how Odysseus built his bed and bedroom? Cite the passage where Odysseus describes his building process.

_____

_____

_____

**3.** Why does Penelope hold back so long before fully accepting the reality of Odysseus's return? What is she afraid of? Use the text to support your conclusions.

_____

_____

_____

**4.** To what is Penelope compared in the epic simile, lines 262–269? How does the language in this passage make her sound similar to Odysseus?

_____

_____

_____

Name _____

Date _____

# Making Connections—Causes and Effects

**Directions:** The slaughter of the suitors is one main event that takes place in the last five books of *The Odyssey*. Decide whether each of the following occurrences is a cause of the suitors' deaths or an effect of their deaths. Write **Cause** or **Effect** on each line below.

_____ 1. The suitors taunt Odysseus, disguised as a beggar.

_____ 2. Odysseus lights a fire to purify the house.

_____ 3. Penelope insists that Odysseus in disguise be given a chance to string the bow.

_____ 4. Athena makes the suitors panic and run down the hall.

_____ 5. The suitors meet the ghosts of Achilles and Agamemnon.

_____ 6. The kinsmen of the suitors hear the rumor that they are dead.

_____ 7. Telemachus puts away the suitors' weapons in a closet.

_____ 8. Melanthius is caught while attempting to get more armor for the suitors.

_____ 9. Members of the suitors' families meet at an assembly.

_____ 10. Zeus decrees that there shall be peace between Odysseus and the suitors' families.

# Creating with the Story Elements

**Directions:** Thinking about the story elements of character, setting, and plot in a novel is very important to understanding what is happening and why. Complete **one** of the following activities based on what you've read so far. Be creative and have fun!

## Characters

Make a Venn or other diagram showing the similarities and differences or connections between Penelope and Odysseus. Add visual elements, such as illustrations or pictures, if you'd like.

## Setting

The ancient Greek setting is central to *The Odyssey*, but what if the story were set in another time and location? How would that change it? Rewrite an episode from the last five books of *The Odyssey*, changing the time period and setting.

## Plot

Pretend to be a sports commentator observing (from a distance) the action that takes place during the contest with the bow or during the fight in the palace. Write a script of your commentary and/or make a recording of it.

Name _____

Date _____

# Post-Reading Theme Thoughts

**Directions:** Read each of the statements in the first column. Choose a main character from *The Odyssey*. Think about that character's point of view. From that character's perspective, decide if the character would agree or disagree with the statements. Record the character's opinion by marking an *X* in Agree or Disagree for each statement. Explain your choices in the fourth column using text evidence.

**Character I Chose:** _____

| Statement | Agree | Disagree | Explain Your Answer |
|---|---|---|---|
| There's no place like home. | | | |
| One of the most important lessons you can learn in life is how to have self-control. | | | |
| Revenge is sweet and sometimes deserved. | | | |
| A clever mind is at least as important as a strong body. | | | |

Name _____

Date _____

# Culminating Activity 1: Create *The Odyssey* Game

**Directions:** Design a game based on the plot and/or characters of *The Odyssey*. Write detailed step-by-step instructions on how to play the game. Some types of games you could create are as follows:

- **Board Game:** Design a board game based on the plot of *The Odyssey* as a whole. This could be a brand new game of your own devising or a special version of an existing board game.

- **Card Game:** Create a deck of Odyssey cards featuring characters and/or scenes from *The Odyssey*. Then, invent a game to play with the cards.

- **Role-playing Game:** Create materials for a dice-based role-playing game in which players take on the roles of various characters from *The Odyssey*.

- **Active Game:** Invent an active game, such as a ball or shuffleboard game, based on some aspect of the plot of *The Odyssey*.

- **Video Game:** Draw designs of the different screens or worlds a viewer might encounter in an Odyssey-based video game. Explain in detail what a player would try to do in each world and at each level of the game.

Name _____

Date _____

# Culminating Activity 2: A Sequel to *The Odyssey*

In Book 23 of *The Odyssey*, lines 299–325, Odysseus mentions to Penelope that he will eventually have to make another journey, as has been foretold by the prophet Tiresias. We can guess from this passage that the ancient Greeks knew and told another story about a later journey taken by Odysseus. Today, however, this other Odysseus story has been lost. All we know of it is what we read in *The Odyssey*.

**Directions:** Create a sequel to *The Odyssey*, based on Odysseus's description of his later journey. Explain in your story why he goes on this journey, who goes with him, how he gets to the distant land described by Tiresias, and why he arrives there carrying an oar. Write an outline for your sequel below.

_____

_____

_____

_____

_____

_____

_____

_____

_____

_____

_____

_____

_____

_____

Name _____

Date _____

# Comprehension Assessment

**Directions:** Circle the best response to each question.

1. Which of the following sentences summarizes a main theme of *The Odyssey*?

    A. Real men never cry.

    B. A heroic death in battle is the best of all possible ways to go.

    C. The gods play no role in causing human misery.

    D. There is no place like home.

2. What quotation from the epic provides the best evidence of your answer?

    E. "It's really not so bad to be a king. All at once/ your palace grows in wealth, your honor grows as well."

    F. "The belly's a shameless dog, there's nothing worse."

    G. "So nothing is as sweet as a man's own country,/ his own parents, even though he's settled down/ in some luxurious house, off in a foreign land."

    H. "By god, I'd rather slave on earth for another man–/ some dirt-poor tenant farmer who scrapes to keep alive–/ than rule down here over all the breathless dead."

3. What is the main idea of this passage?

    They threw themselves in the labor, rowed on fast/ but once we'd plowed the breakers twice as far,/ again I began to taunt the Cyclops—men around me trying to check me, calm me, left and right:/ "So headstrong—why? Why rile the beast again?"

    _____

    _____

4. Choose **two** details to support your answer to number 3.

    A. Odysseus foolishly shouts out his name to the Cyclops.

    B. The Cyclops lives in a cave, not in a palace or a house.

    C. The Cyclops is a giant with one eye who likes to eat humans.

    D. The Cyclops prays to Poseidon to punish Odysseus for blinding him.

# Comprehension Assessment (cont.)

5.  Which statement best expresses the reason Penelope secretly unweaves Laertes's shroud?

    E.  She is dissatisfied with her work.

    F.  She wants to buy time so she won't have to choose a new husband.

    G.  She needs the yarn for other weaving projects.

    H.  Penelope has given up on the possibility that Odysseus might return home.

6.  What is the significance of the episode from *The Odyssey* described below?

    [A]nd charging up to the hunt he stopped, at bay–/ and Odysseus rushed him first,/ shaking his long spear in a sturdy hand,/ wild to strike but the boar struck faster,/ lunging in on the slant, a tusk thrusting up/ over the boy's knee, gouging a deep strip of flesh…

    _____

    _____

7.  Which statement best expresses a reoccurring theme from *The Odyssey*?

    A.  We should provide food, shelter, and hospitality to strangers in need.

    B.  Eat, drink, be merry, and don't worry about the consequences.

    C.  Twenty years is too long to expect someone to wait for you.

    D.  We should tell the truth straightaway and at all times.

8.  What quotation below provides support for your answer to number 7?

    E.  Odysseus: "From all who walk the earth our bards deserve/ esteem and awe, for the Muse herself has taught them/ paths of song.  She loves the breed of harpers."

    F.  Medon: "Now the suitors are plotting something worse,/harsher, crueler . . . / They're poised to cut Telemachus down with bronze swords/ on his way back home."

    G.  The Sirens: "Come closer, famous Odysseus. . . / moor your ship on our coast so you can hear our song!"

    H.  Echenus: "This is no way, Alcinous.  How indecent, look,/ our guest on the ground, in the ashes by the fire!/ . . . Come, raise him up and set the stranger now,/ in a silver-studded chair."

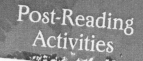
# Response to Literature: A Voyage of Self-Discovery?

Odysseus makes a very long voyage home in Homer's *The Odyssey*, but is this just a voyage across oceans and through strange lands? Or is Odysseus's voyage also a voyage of self-discovery?

**Directions:** In a carefully crafted written response, argue either that Odysseus changes and grows as a result of his many harrowing experiences or that he remains the same Odysseus throughout these experiences. Cite ample evidence from Homer's epic to support your opinion.

_____

_____

_____

_____

_____

_____

_____

_____

_____

_____

_____

_____

_____

_____

Name _____

Date _____

# Response to Literature Rubric

**Directions:** Use this rubric to evaluate student responses.

| | Exceptional Writing | Quality Writing | Developing Writing |
|---|---|---|---|
| **Focus and Organization** | ☐ States a clear opinion and elaborates well. Engages the reader from the opening hook through the middle to the conclusion. Demonstrates clear understanding of the intended audience and purpose of the piece. | ☐ Provides a clear and consistent opinion. Maintains a clear perspective and supports it through elaborating details. Makes the opinion clear in the opening hook and summarizes well in the conclusion. | ☐ Provides an inconsistent point of view. Does not support the topic adequately or misses pertinent information. Provides lack of clarity in the beginning, middle, and conclusion. |
| **Text Evidence** | ☐ Provides comprehensive and accurate support. Includes relevant and worthwhile text references. | ☐ Provides limited support. Provides few supporting text references. | ☐ Provides very limited support for the text. Provides no supporting text references. |
| **Written Expression** | ☐ Uses descriptive and precise language with clarity and intention. Maintains a consistent voice and uses an appropriate tone that supports meaning. Uses multiple sentence types and transitions well between ideas. | ☐ Uses a broad vocabulary. Maintains a consistent voice and supports a tone and feelings through language. Varies sentence length and word choices. | ☐ Uses a limited and unvaried vocabulary. Provides an inconsistent or weak voice and tone. Provides little to no variation in sentence type and length. |
| **Language Conventions** | ☐ Capitalizes, punctuates, and spells accurately. Demonstrates complete thoughts within sentences, with accurate subject-verb agreement. Uses paragraphs appropriately and with clear purpose. | ☐ Capitalizes, punctuates, and spells accurately. Demonstrates complete thoughts within sentences and appropriate grammar. Paragraphs are properly divided and supported. | ☐ Incorrectly capitalizes, punctuates, and spells. Uses fragmented or run-on sentences. Utilizes poor grammar overall. Paragraphs are poorly divided and developed. |

The responses provided here are just examples of what the students may answer. Many accurate responses are possible for the questions throughout this unit.

**During-Reading Vocabulary Activity—Section 1:**
**Books 1–4** (page 16)

1. Two eagles soar over the crowd together and then begin to attack each other. Halitherses interprets this as a sign that Odysseus will soon be home and that disaster is coming for the suitors (Book 2, lines 165–174).

2. The kings feed Telemachus. They do this before asking him questions about himself. Menelaus gives him the best cut of the meat (Book 3, lines 72–73). The kings also offer shelter and gifts.

**Close Reading the Literature—Section 1:**
**Books 1–4** (page 21)

1. The suitors are playing with dice and lounging on ox hides (line 124). Servants are rushing around preparing them food and wine.

2. Telemachus is daydreaming that his father might arrive and drive out the suitors (lines 134–137). We can tell from this that he doesn't like the suitors or what is going on in his home. He misses his father and feels unable to change the situation on his own.

3. Telemachus rushes to let the stranger in (line 140), gives her a chair of honor (line 152), and puts off asking her questions until after she has been given something to eat.

4. Students may say the suitors seem like "party boys," or something similar. The suitors are described as "swaggering" (line 124), which makes them sound egotistical and self-assured. From the action of the attendants (line 127 on), we can see that they are used to being waited on, from which students might conclude that the suitors are rich, lazy, or spoiled.

**Making Connections—Section 1:**
**Books 1–4** (page 22)

Students' responses will vary. The objects are used by the following characters in the text.

- chariot—used by Telemachus and Pisistratus
- distaff—used by Penelope and the other women of the palace
- loom—used by Penelope and the other women
- lyre—used by Phemius the bard
- mixing-bowl—given to Telemachus by Menelaus
- set of smith's tools—used by the smith preparing the heifer for sacrifice
- ship—used by Telemachus and an all-male crew
- spindle—said to belong to Helen
- storage skins—used by Telemachus
- tripod—gifted to Telemachus by Menelaus

**During-Reading Vocabulary Activity—Section 2:**
**Books 5–9** (page 26)

1. Calypso is a **nymph**. She is immortal and has the ability to make Odysseus immortal, too (Book 5, lines 230–231). She eats the food of the gods (nectar and ambrosia), instead of ordinary food (Book 5, lines 103–104).

2. Odysseus requests a **convoy** from the Phaeacian queen, Arete (Book 7, lines 179–180), and her husband, Alcinous. Odysseus is without a ship and crew and has no way to get home.

**Close Reading the Literature—Section 2:**
**Books 5–9** (page 31)

1. The neighbors do not come because the Cyclops cries that "Nobody" was killing him (lines 454–460). Odysseus had previously claimed that his name was "Nobody."

2. Odysseus shows cleverness, leadership ability, and the ability to get out of tight situations when he hides himself and his men under the bellies of the sheep. This allows the men to get out of the cave without being detected by the blind Cyclops (lines 477–515).

3. Odysseus taunts the Cyclops (line 430 on), although his men do not approve of this behavior and try to get him to stop (lines 548–557). The language of the men indicates that they are fearful for their lives.

4. Once the Cyclops learns Odysseus's name, he is able to direct his father, Poseidon, to take revenge on Odysseus (lines 584–595). Odysseus let his pride and anger get the better of him in this instance (lines 556–562). He loses self-control.

**Making Connections—Section 2:**
**Books 5–9** (page 32)

1. Odysseus's joy on seeing the shore; joy children feel when their sick father gets well.

2. pebbles stuck in an octopus's suckers; strips of Odysseus's skin stuck to the rocks

3. a burning brand or coal buried in ash; Odysseus buried in leaves

4. Artemis; Nausicaa

5. Odysseus; mountain lion

6. a person's stomach; a begging dog

7. Odysseus in tears; a woman crying for her killed husband

8. a blacksmith's ax or adze plunged in cold water; the stake in the Cyclops's eye

**Close Reading the Literature—Section 3:**
**Books 10–14** (page 41)

1. Odysseus drops his stick and sinks low to the ground as the dogs attack (lines 33–34), which indicates both that he knows about dog behavior and can think on his feet. Odysseus is clearly not the master of his own estate right now, as the dogs view him as an outsider and a threat. Eumaeus shows great alarm over the possibility of a guest or suppliant being harmed (lines 40–42). His words indicate that he is someone who cares about the welfare of others and believes in the importance of following proper guest-host protocol.

2. Eumaeus declares himself heartbroken over the loss of Odysseus (line 44) and over the state of his master's estate. He praises Odysseus highly, describing him as a "kind lord" (line 74). He states his belief that Odysseus would have gifted him with a house, land, and a wife, had he not disappeared (lines 72–74).

3. Eumaeus has a very low opinion of the suitors. He calls them "brazen rascals" (line 106). He complains of how they devour all of Odysseus's goods and that they don't "do their courting fairly" (line 104).

4. Eumaeus shares his culture's belief that "every stranger and beggar comes from Zeus" (line 66) and thus has special rights. He uses his own bedding to make a seat for his visitor. He feeds the visitor first before asking him to tell his story.

**Making Connections—Section 3:**
**Books 10–14** (page 42)

1. Dawn; 2. Hermes; 3. Odysseus; 4. Alcinous; 5. Achilles; 6. Scylla; 7. Zeus; 8 Poseidon; 9. Athena; 10. Telemachus

**During-Reading Vocabulary Activity—Section 4:**
**Books 15–19** (page 46)

1. Telemachus is worried that the suitors are eating up his herds and flocks and that they wish to take control of his land and palace, as well.

2. The suitors are always eating, drinking, playing games, and listening to music. They never seem to do any work.

**Close Reading the Literature—Section 4:**
**Books 15–19** (page 51)

1. Eurycleia identifies Odysseus by the scar on his leg. He is clearly very dear to her. We learn in this passage that Eurycleia knew and cared for Odysseus as a baby (see line 455). When she recognizes him, she is overjoyed and begins to cry (lines 533–534).

2. Odysseus received the scar while visiting his grandfather as a boy. He was gouged in the leg by a wild boar while out hunting. The wounding is described on lines 501–514.

3. Students may conclude that Odysseus was bold, brave, and perhaps not cautious enough, based on the fact that he was first to rush the boar (line 506).

4. Students may conclude that Odysseus has changed. They may say that he seems more cautious and self-controlled now, basing their conclusion on the fact that he did not rush directly home to challenge the suitors. Instead of rushing to action, the older Odysseus bides his time and uses strategy.

**Close Reading the Literature—Section 5:**
**Books 20–24** (page 61)

1. In Book 23 lines 197–198, Penelope tells Eurycleia to move the bed out of the bedroom. It is a test because the real Odysseus will know that the bed can't be moved.

2. Odysseus describes how he made the bed from the trunk of a still-rooted olive tree and then built the bedroom around this tree-bed in lines 214–229.

3. Penelope tells Odysseus that she has been afraid for years that someone might come and trick her by claiming to be her husband (lines 242–250). She has not wanted to commit adultery like Helen.

4. Penelope is compared to a shipwrecked sailor now on solid ground again. Though she has only figuratively been at sea and shipwrecked, whereas Odysseus literally has, both spouses have in a sense been adrift since their life together was wrecked.

**Making Connections—Section 5:**
**Books 20–24** (page 62)

1. cause; 2. effect; 3. cause; 4. cause; 5. effect; 6. effect; 7. cause; 8. cause; 9. effect; 10. effect

**Comprehension Assessment** (pages 67–68)

1. D. There is no place like home.

2. G. "So nothing is as sweet as a man's own country,/ his own parents, even though he's settled down/ in some luxurious house, off in a foreign land."

3. Main Idea: It is important to maintain self-control or keep one's pride in check.

4. Supporting Details: A. Odysseus foolishly shouts out his name to the Cyclops; D. The Cyclops prays to Poseidon to punish Odysseus for blinding him.

5. F. She wants to buy time so she won't have to choose a new husband.

6. The episode is significant because it was during this childhood episode that Odysseus received his scar, which later proves his identity. The episode is also significant because Odysseus acted impulsively and may have learned from this event that it is important to wait and have self-control.

7. A. We should provide food, shelter, and hospitality to strangers in need.

8. H. Echenus: "This is no way, Alcinous. How indecent, look,/ our guest on the ground, in the ashes by the fire!/ . . . Come raise him up and set the stranger now,/ in a silver-studded chair."